BRIDGING THE ENERGY GAP

Andrew Langley

Raintree

Chicago, Illinois

EXPRESS EDITION

www.heinemannraintree.com
Visit our website to find out more information about Heinemann-Raintree books.

To order:
☎ Phone 888-454-2279
💻 Visit www.heinemannraintree.com to browse our catalog and order online.

Edited by Andrew Farrow and Adrian Vigliano
Designed by Victoria Allen
Original illustrations © Capstone Global Library Ltd.
Illustrated by Tower Designs UK Limited
Picture research by Mica Brancic
Production by Eirian Griffiths
Originated by Capstone Global Library
Printed and bound in the United States of America by Corporate Graphics in North Mankato, Minnesota.

15 14 13 12 11
10 9 8 7 6 5 4 3 2 1

Library of Congress Cataloging-in-Publication Data
Cataloging-in-Publication data is on file at the Library of Congress.

ISBNs: 978-1-4109-4318-7 (HC); 978-1-4109-4325-5 (PB)

Acknowledgments
The author and publishers are grateful to the following for permission to reproduce copyright material: Corbis p. 4 © Rudy Sulgan. p. 20 © Ed Kashi, p. 22 epa/Pool/© Sebastian Derungs, p. 23 © Karen Kasmauski, p. 25 © Francesco Acerbis, p. 26 © Cameron Davidson, p. 29 epa/© Song Jianchun, p. 30 © Layne Kennedy, p. 31 Robert Harding World Imagery/© David Lomax, p. 32 Science Faction/© Peter Ginter, p. 35 epa/© Alex Hofford, p. 36 Reuters/© Brian Snyder, p. 41 Aurora Photos/© Peter Essick; Getty Images p. 5 U.S. Coast Guard, p. 7 Taxi/Allan Shoemake, p. 10 Photographer's Choice/Lester Lefkowitz, p. 11 Bloomberg/Norm Betts, p. 12 Hulton Archive/Fox Photos, p. 15 AFP Photo/Frederic J. Brown, p. 17 Spencer Platt, p. 33 David McNew, p. 34 AFP Photo/Frederick Florin, p. 37 Tim Graham, p. 38 Eco Images/Universal Images Group p. 39 Visuals Unlimited, Inc./Ashley Cooper, p. 40 AFP Photo DDP/Hero Lang; Reuters p. 8 © Krishnendu Halder; Science Photo Library p. 19 David Nunik; Shutterstock p. 24 © John Carnemolla, p. 18 © Philip Lange.

Cover photograph of a resident collecting pieces of wood washed ashore in front of wind turbines in the Philippines used with permission of Reuters/© Cheryl Ravelo.

We would like to thank Michael D. Mastrandrea, Ph.D., for his invaluable help in the preparation of this book.

Every effort has been made to contact copyright holders of any material reproduced in this book. Any omissions will be rectified in subsequent printings if notice is given to the publisher.

Disclaimer
All the Internet addresses (URLs) given in this book were valid at the time of going to press. However, due to the dynamic nature of the Internet, some addresses may have changed, or sites may have changed or ceased to exist since publication. While the author and publisher regret any inconvenience this may cause readers, no responsibility for any such changes can be accepted by either the author or the publisher.

Contents

Words appearing in the text in bold, **like this**, are explained in the glossary.

Powering the World

Energy is all around us. It powers our lights and gadgets. Energy also heats our homes. There are many kinds of energy outdoors, such as wind power and the heat of the Sun.

Energy at work

So, what is energy? It is the ability to do work. Energy is what keeps our world working. In **power stations**, the energy from **fuels** such as coal and oil is released. This produces supplies of **electricity**. Electricity powers machines, streetlights, and more. Other kinds of fuel, such as gasoline and diesel, drive aircraft, trucks, and cars.

Modern cities use a huge amount of energy. In the form of electricity, this energy lights up places like New York City.

The energy gap

But this way of living cannot go on forever. Why not?

1. There is a limited supply of important materials such as coal and oil. When we have used these supplies up, there will be no more.

2. When coal or oil burn, they release a substance called **carbon** into the air. The amount of carbon in the air is rising rapidly. It is the major cause of a dangerous rise in the world's temperatures. This is known as **global warming**.

These problems are growing fast. Soon, they may create an "**energy gap**." This means we will not be able to produce enough power to meet our energy needs.

Solving the problem

We are already using other sources of energy that will never run out. Examples of these kinds of energy include flowing water, the wind, and the Sun. But will these be enough? This book will help you explore the options. You can make your own decisions about how to bridge the energy gap.

Smoke and flames rise above the water. Oil was being removed from under the ocean. Accidents like this can cause a lot of damage.

WORD BANK

electricity   form of energy that power machines, streetlights, and more
energy   ability to do work
energy gap   situation in which we cannot produce enough power for our needs
global warming   rise in the temperature of Earth

5

The energy chain

Most sources of **energy** occur naturally. Coal, oil, and **natural gas** lie underground. (Natural gas is a **fuel gas**. A gas is a substance with no shape, like air.) Wind, water, and sunshine are above ground. But we cannot use them directly. For example, how could you power your computer with a lump of coal? These energy sources have to be turned into energy we can use.

Creating usable energy

Coal, oil, and natural gas have to be carried long distances to places called **power stations**. There, they can be turned into usable forms of energy. To use wind power, giant **turbines** have to be built. Turbines are giant machines that are turned by the wind. This creates **electricity**.

Coal, oil, and natural gas are carried long distances to power stations. There, they are turned into usable fuels.

The energy then has to be provided to people who need it. Look in the street. Can you see power lines carrying electricity? Or covers in the road where gas and water pipes run beneath your feet? All this requires a lot of work—and money.

Electricity is sent to people along power lines like these.

WORD BANK

chemical energy   energy made by burning—for example, by burning coal
kinetic energy   energy made by movement, such as wind or waves
potential energy   energy made by using natural forms of energy that are stored—
         for example, water kept behind a dam or barrier
turbine   machine turned by flowing energy that turns energy into electricity

7

A growing world

The world's **population** (number of people) is growing at an amazing speed. Some experts guess that it will reach 8.5 billion people by 2025. In countries such as China and India, many new factories, towns, and transportation systems are also being built. This growth means that more and more **energy** will be needed in years to come.

Many countries have recently seen an increase in the number of cars—and traffic jams.

How long will our resources last?

The pie chart on the right shows how much we depend on oil, coal, and **natural gas** to create energy. These three energy sources are called **fossil fuels**. They make up more than three-quarters of the world's energy.

But where do fossil fuels come from? They began as the remains of ancient plants and animals. (The remains are called **fossils**.) Over millions of years, these fossils were crushed underground. They changed into fossil fuels.

But when are these materials going to run out? Nobody knows the answer to this question. One expert, Hermann-Josef Wagner, thinks that oil will last 40 to 50 more years. He says that coal will last 180 to 240 more years. He thinks that natural gas will last 50 to 60 more years.

A global energy pie chart

A pie chart is a simple way to show how a total is divided up into parts. In a pie chart, a circle represents the total. It looks like a pie, with each part becoming a slice of the whole. This pie chart shows about how much of each kind of energy source the world uses.

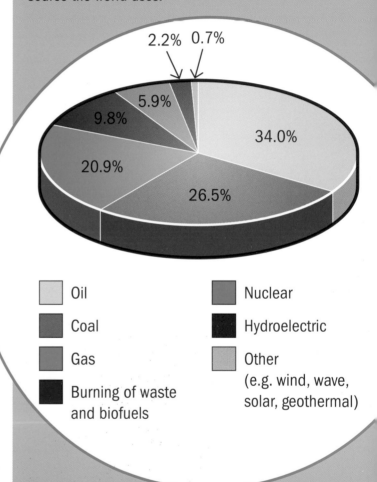

Oil — 34.0%
Coal — 26.5%
Gas — 20.9%
Burning of waste and biofuels — 9.8%
Nuclear — 5.9%
Hydroelectric — 2.2%
Other (e.g. wind, wave, solar, geothermal) — 0.7%

You can get lots of information on energy. Look on the website of the International Energy Authority at www.iea.org. Click on "Statistics," then "Key statistics."

Where Does Energy Come From?

All **energy** has to be released from a source, such as coal or oil. But how were these energy sources made in the first place? The answer is simple: they used the energy of the Sun. The Sun sends out an amazing and endless supply of energy.

Fireball in the sky

The **rays** (lines or beams of energy) of the Sun send energy to plants. This helps them grow. We eat the plants and use the energy in them to run our bodies. We also burn some plants to create heat (see page 36).

Coal and oil also contain the Sun's energy. They are made of **fossils** that have been heated by the Sun over millions of years.

The Sun's heat causes wind and rain. It makes rivers flow. We can use the power from the wind, rain, and flowing rivers for our energy needs.

Coal is dug out from underground. It is one of the most important fossil fuels.

Some sources of **fuel** have to be changed before they can be burned. Equipment at this station removes oil from oil sands.

Fossil or renewable?

Fossil fuels like coal and oil formed long ago, deep inside Earth. Once we use them up, there will not be any more of them. They are not **renewable**. We cannot make new supplies.

But there are plenty of energy resources that *are* renewable. The Sun will shine for millions of years. Winds will always blow. Rivers and seas will always move. We can continue **harnessing** (using) their power for as long as we want.

WORD BANK

harness   use the power of something
renewable   fuel or material that can be grown or made again
solar energy   energy from the Sun

A brief history of energy

Humans have used the world's **energy** for thousands of years. Until about 300 years ago, this meant **renewable** sources, such as firewood, wind, and water.

Then came the **Industrial Revolution**. This was a period in history from the late 1700s through the 1800s. It happened in countries like Great Britain and the United States. Factories and new kinds of machinery came into use. These new inventions needed much more power. Coal became the most important **fuel**.

Then, about 150 years ago, people discovered how to turn oil into fuel. Soon gasoline and oil were being burned in cars, trains, and **power stations**. **Natural gas** was often found underground with oil. This became another major energy source. It was used for things like home heating and cooking.

Carbon crisis

But the amazing rise of these fuels has caused major problems. When these fuels are burned, the substance **carbon** is released Most carbon forms the **gas carbon dioxide**.

Carbon dioxide is a major cause of **climate change**. This is a change in the world's weather patterns, such as rain or heat. The graph on page 13 shows how carbon dioxide levels have increased over time.

During the Industrial Revolution, coal was burned to power steam trains.

Where are the main energy sources . . . ?

As we already seen, over 75 percent of all the world's energy is created from **fossil fuels**—coal, oil, and natural gas. But these fuels are only found in certain places.

Renewable energy is different. Generally speaking, water, wind, and **solar energy** (Sun energy) can be found anywhere. Still, some regions have faster rivers, more wind, and stronger sunlight than others. Look at the map at the top of page 14. This shows which countries are using these energy sources.

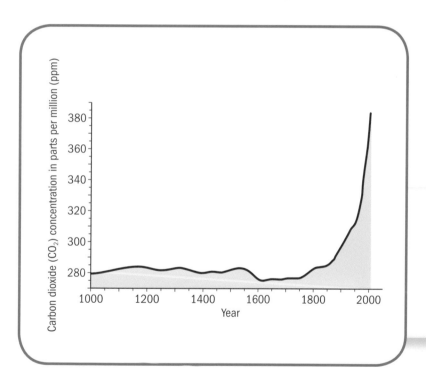

This graph shows the levels of carbon dioxide over the last 1,000 years.

Compare the two maps below. In the top map, "**clean energy**" means **energy** sources that are **renewable**. They also do not release much **carbon**. The colors in this map help you see which countries use the most clean energy. The bottom map shows which countries burn the most **fossil fuels**. In the past, poorer regions did not burn many fossil fuels. This has changed in recent years. Many of these countries are now expanding their factories and transportation systems. This requires a lot of energy.

Clean energy as a percentage of world energy use in 2006

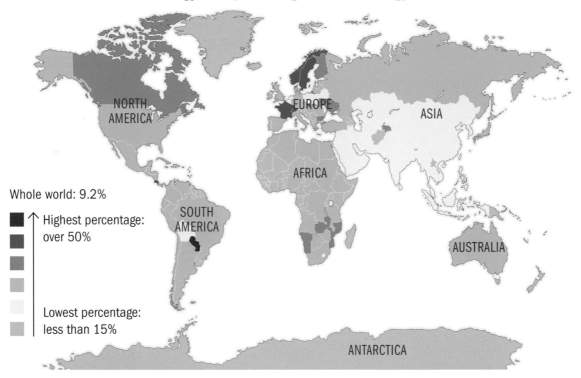

NORTH AMERICA

EUROPE

ASIA

AFRICA

SOUTH AMERICA

AUSTRALIA

Whole world: 9.2%

↑ Highest percentage: over 50%

Lowest percentage: less than 15%

ANTARCTICA

Fossil fuel use as a percentage of world energy use in 2006

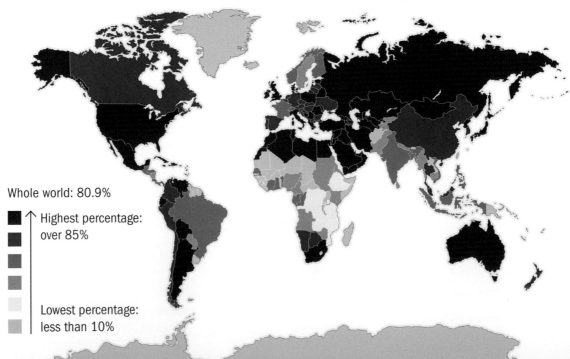

Whole world: 80.9%

↑ Highest percentage: over 85%

Lowest percentage: less than 10%

Pollution in China

Since the 1900s, by far the biggest users of energy have been wealthy countries such as the United States, Germany, Great Britain, and Japan. The United States, for example, contains only about 5 percent of the world's **population**. Yet it has used 26 percent of the world's energy.

But today, China uses a lot of coal. It uses more coal than the United States and the European Union (a group of 27 countries in Europe) combined. It does so to keep up with its people's growing need for factories, **power stations**, and transportation systems.

Burning all this coal causes air **pollution** (poisonous or dangerous substances in the air). This affects the health of people in China. It also affects people elsewhere. Clouds of pollution are spreading across the Pacific Ocean to the United States.

China is working to find ways to clean up its **gas emissions** (the dirty gas given off). But the country must struggle to find a way to grow and develop at the same time.

Coal burned in power stations produces gases that are dangerous to health.

WORD BANK

clean energy   energy source that is renewable and causes little damage to the environment
emission   giving off of dirty gases or other materials
pollution   harming the environment with poisonous or dangerous substances

Fossil Fuels

Coal, oil, and **natural gas** play important roles in our lives. Just think of the things we probably would not have without them. We would not have cars, **electricity**, heating, air travel, and more. But we know that burning these **fossil fuels** is causing **global warming**. Is there any way to make them safer and longer-lasting?

King coal

The use of coal has brought **energy** and wealth to many parts of the world. There are two types of coal. Hard coal is black. It gives out lots of energy when burned. Brown coal is softer. It contains less energy. Both have to be dug out of the ground. Sometimes they are dug from areas deep within Earth called **mines**. Coal mining is hard and dangerous work.

Can we make coal clean?

When burned, coal releases **carbon** and other dangerous substances. These substances cause **pollution**. But scientists are developing a system called **Carbon Capture and Storage (CCS)**. In this system, **carbon dioxide** is taken out of waste **gases** from coal **power stations**. It is then pumped deep underground and stored.

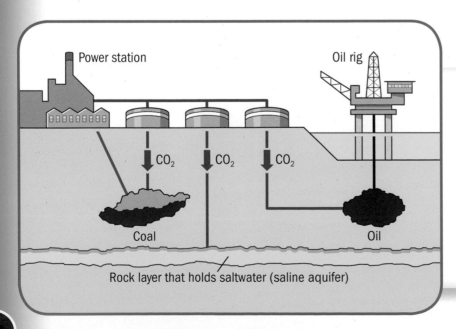

Power station
Oil rig
CO_2 CO_2 CO_2
Coal
Oil
Rock layer that holds saltwater (saline aquifer)

Some people believe carbon dioxide (CO_2) from power stations can be stored underground. But is there room for it all?

Still, many people argue that CCS has not been proven to work. It is still very new and needs to be tested more. They feel that people should instead try not to use as many fossil fuels.

Cutting and moving coal out of a mine is a difficult and dangerous job.

CASE STUDY

The West Virginia mine disaster

On April 5, 2010, a huge explosion killed 29 miners at the Upper Big Branch coal mine in the state of West Virginia. The explosion led to many questions about mine safety. You can find out more about this story by going to http://www.cnn.com and searching for "West Virginia mining disaster." Then think more about the dangers miners face every day.

WORD BANK
mine area deep within Earth where people dig for substances such as coal

Oil from the rock

Oil is the most important **energy** source in the world. This **fossil fuel** can be used as **fuel** for vehicles and **power stations**. It can also be used to make a wide range of substances, including plastics and grease for machines.

Oil is found deep underground in rock or sand. Many of these oil **deposits** (stores) are under the sea. Oil companies have to drill from special floating platforms.

Black gold

The many uses of oil make it very valuable. Countries such as Saudi Arabia, Iran, and Venezuela became very wealthy thanks to their oil deposits. Today, oil discoveries are boosting other countries, including Nigeria, Libya, Indonesia, and Malaysia.

This is Dubai, which is part of the United Arab Emirates. Because of its oil deposits, it has become very wealthy.

Oil pollution

Scraping Bottom
By Robert Kunzig

Alberta, Canada—Once considered too expensive, as well as too damaging to the land, [mining in] Alberta's oil sands is now a gamble worth billions.

Nowhere on Earth is more earth being moved these days than in the Athabasca Valley. To **extract** [remove] each barrel of oil from a surface mine, the industry must first cut down the forest, then remove an average of two tons [1.8 tonnes] of peat and dirt that lie above the oil sands layer, then two tons of the sand itself.

The passage to the left is from a magazine article in *National Geographic*, in March 2009. The writer was reporting about another way to get oil. Tar sands, or oil sands, are areas of sand soaked in oil. Removing this oil is expensive and messy. It does a lot of damage to forest areas. But it makes billions of dollars. Do you think getting oil is worth the damage caused to the **environment** (our natural surroundings)?

Can you find out about other places where attempts to get oil have damaged the environment? For example, research the *Deepwater Horizon* explosion of April 2010. This greatly damaged the Gulf of Mexico.

It takes lots of water to get the oil from tar sand. The dirty water is then stored in special ponds.

Natural gas

Natural gas is usually found wherever there are other **fossil fuels**. It is piped to the surface and cleaned. Then it is piped to **gas power stations** and to our homes. We use it for heating and cooking.

Natural gas should be the cleanest of the fossil fuels. This is because it releases much less **carbon** when it is burned than other fossil fuels do. But a lot of unburned gas gets accidentally leaked into the air. This can cause even more damage than waste fumes.

Energy into food

The **energy** from natural gas can be turned into another important material: **fertilizer**. After treatment, the gas becomes a solid. It is sprinkled on farmland in the form of tiny white grains. This makes plants grow fast and strong. This kind of fertilizer has changed farming. More food crops can be grown than before on the same area of land. In this way, fossil fuels are helping to feed the world.

But there is a downside. The fertilizers are being washed out of the soil by rain. They are then spread, poisoning rivers and ponds.

Some energy companies simply burn the natural gas that they find with oil. This woman cooks food near the flames to protest against the waste.

If you were in charge of your country's energy, would you continue burning fossil fuels? After all, coal, oil, and natural gas are there to be used. Or should we stop using fossil fuels altogether, because of the damage they cause to the **environment**? If not, what should we do instead? Lay out your evidence using a concept web like the one below.

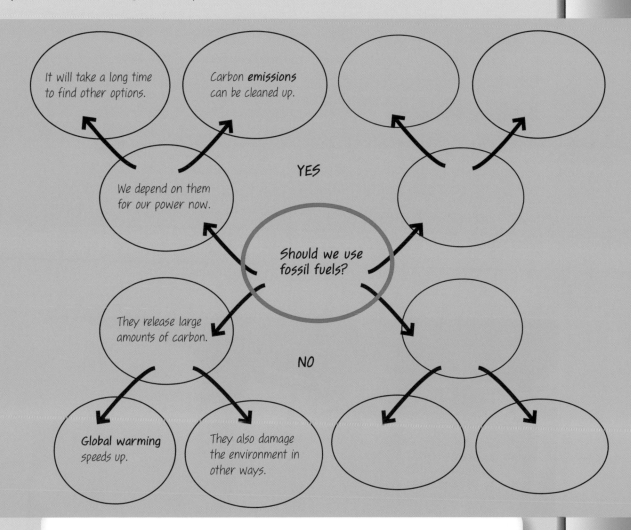

A concept web helps you to arrange your evidence. At the center of the web (like a spider) is the main question. Arrows from this point outward. They link to boxes that contain possible answers. Copy and fill out a concept web like the one above.

The Mighty Atom

Nuclear energy is the most powerful of all **energy** sources. It is created by splitting special **atoms**. (Atoms are the tiny units that make up everything on Earth.) This splitting can create an enormous amount of energy.

Nuclear energy has been used to make the most terrible weapons in history. Nuclear bombs destroyed Japanese cities in 1945, during World War II (1939–45). It can also be used to create cheap and clean power. But how safe is it?

Splitting the atom

A nuclear **power station** uses the energy inside **uranium** atoms. The **nucleus** (central part) of a uranium atom is split in two. This releases great heat. The heat makes steam. This steam creates **electricity**.

A nuclear power station needs very little **fuel**. Nuclear power also does not release any **carbon dioxide** or other waste.

Scientists check the air near nuclear power stations.

What are the dangers of nuclear power?

Yet nuclear energy poses big safety problems. For example, at Chernobyl, Ukraine, in 1986, a nuclear station was destroyed in an accident. Deadly **radiation** leaked out into the air. Radiation is energy in the form of **rays** (lines or beams). This caused sickness and death for people nearby.

Nuclear power also produces dangerous waste material. So, it is sealed in tanks and buried deep underground. But it will remain **radioactive** (give off dangerous radiation) for thousands of years. It could be harmful to animals and plants.

Many of the materials used to create nuclear power become dangerously radioactive. They have to be handled and stored very carefully.

WORD BANK

atom smallest unit that makes up everything on Earth

nuclear energy energy made by splitting the nucleus (central part) of a uranium atom

radiation energy in the form of rays (lines or beams)

Where does uranium come from?

Uranium, like coal, has to be **mined** from under Earth's surface. Then, it has to be crushed and cleaned. These processes can cause great damage to the **environment**.

The biggest producers of uranium are the countries Canada and Australia. Other countries with large **deposits** include Kazakhstan, Russia, and Nigeria. As **nuclear energy** becomes more important, many countries will want to get uranium from these areas.

Uranium mines like this one leave huge holes in the ground. They cause damage to the environment that surrounds it.

Nuclear power and France

In the 1990s, the country of France decided that nuclear energy would be its main source for **electricity**. It set out plans to try to make nuclear energy as safe and effective as possible.

Today, France's nuclear **power stations** provide about 80 percent of the country's electricity. That means France releases fewer harmful substances, like **carbon dioxide**, than many other countries. It also has less of a need for oil. But France has still not solved the problems of what to do with nuclear waste.

Are the French right? What would you do if you lived in a country with few **fuel** resources? Would you risk building nuclear power stations?

Some countries, such as France, are planning to build many new nuclear power stations.

WORD BANK
uranium substance that is used to create nuclear reactions

Wind Power and Waterpower

Winds, rivers, seas, and waterfalls are all sources of **energy**. They will always be available in nature. They are **renewable** resources.

Back to nature

For most of history, people made machines called windmills and water mills. These could **harness** the power of wind and water. But during the **Industrial Revolution**, the use of coal and oil produced much more power. This power was also more reliable and quick. As a result, windmills and water mills became less popular. But today, new kinds of windmills and water mills are being designed. This avoids the problems of burning **fossil fuels**.

Many wind farms are built in the sea, near land. The wind speed stays fairly constant in these areas.

Blowing power

How do people turn wind into **electricity**? The first stage is to make the wind turn a giant fan called a wind **turbine**. Inside the turbine is a machine called a **generator**. This produces electricity. In wind farms, many turbines are usually grouped together. The power they produce is fed into a central source of electricity, called a **grid**. This grid sends out energy to everyone in a large area. Some wind farms cover huge areas of land.

Is it worth it?

Some scientists believe wind turbines cannot create enough energy to replace **power stations**. Currently these turbines provide only about 2 percent of the world's electricity.

Another big problem is that wind does not blow all the time or at the same speed. And some parts of the world get much less wind than others. Some people also think that wind farms are ugly and ruin the appearance of beautiful scenery.

What would YOU do ?

Imagine the government plans to build a big new wind farm near your home. Your region will no longer have to depend on electricity created in a coal-fired power station. Is this a good thing?

Make a list of possible reasons for and against wind power. For example:

For	Against
It will make power cheaper.	Or will it make power more expensive?
Wind will not run out.	The turbines will make a lot of noise.

Use research to find more about this issue. Add your own ideas.

WORD BANK

generator machine that produces electricity
grid central source of electricity that sends it to everyone in a large area

27

Falling water

The power of moving water can be used to turn a **turbine**. This creates **electricity**. This form of **energy** is called **hydroelectric energy**. It is **renewable**. The countries Canada, Brazil, and Norway produce nearly half of their electricity from waterpower.

Hydroelectric energy has many benefits. It does not create any air **pollution**. It is reliable, because water flows at a regular rate. Hydroelectric **power stations** last longer than other power stations. Best of all, waterpower can be used for big or small energy needs.

But hydroelectric power can also create problems. **Dams** must be built on rivers. These are structures that hold back the energy of the moving water. But damming rivers can destroy animals' natural surroundings. Also, having less water flowing downstream can threaten fish and other forms of life.

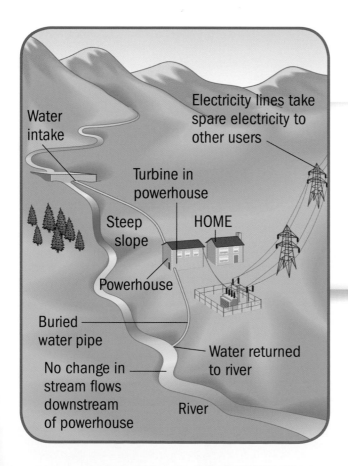

Water intake

Electricity lines take spare electricity to other users

Turbine in powerhouse

Steep slope

HOME

Powerhouse

Buried water pipe

No change in stream flows downstream of powerhouse

Water returned to river

River

This diagram shows how running water is directed into a small stream. This stream flows to a power station.

The Three Gorges Dam

The country of China desperately needs more electricity. This will help its towns and businesses grow. But we have already seen how burning coal can cause major problems for the **environment** (see page 15). So, the Chinese government is trying to find better ways to make power.

Construction of the Three Gorges Dam started in 1992. This dam was built across the Yangtze River. The dam provides hydroelectric energy. But the huge amount of water held behind the dam rises and falls. As a result, there are serious landslides, when areas of surrounding earth wash away. Water pollution is also a problem. So, the area near the dam is probably unsafe for people to live in. About 1.2 million people have already been forced to leave their homes. Hundreds of thousands more must be moved.

What can be done about the pollution and the problems caused for so many people? How else could the Chinese have tackled their energy problem?

The huge Three Gorges Dam is nearly 1.5 miles (2.3 kilometers) long.

WORD BANK

dam   structure that holds back the flow of water

hydroelectric energy   form of energy created when the power of moving water is used to turn a turbine and create electricity

Waves and tides

The sea is always moving. There are waves on the surface. This up-and-down movement could be turned into **energy** we can use. Most parts of the ocean also have rising and falling motions called **tides**. The natural flow of tides back and forth could be used. This could then turn **turbines**. Scientists are looking into the best ways to use the energy of waves and tides.

The sea is a natural source of power. Yet so far, we have not found a good way to use its energy.

Developing renewables

At the moment, **renewable** sources provide only a tiny part of the world's energy. Why is this? For a start, **fossil fuels** are easier to use. This is because the existing power system has been built up around them. Also, they produce a lot of power. So, energy companies have spent their money in **mines**, oil fields, and **power stations**. They have spent very little money on researching renewable sources.

This will have to change if we want to bridge the coming **energy gap**. If we are going to use fewer fossil fuels, renewable energies will have to fill the gap. Scientists will need to think of cheaper and more **efficient** (effective, yet not wasteful) methods of using wind and water.

The new rise of British sea power

In 2008 a strange, 37-meter- (122-foot-) long device set off from a dock in Northern Ireland. The device, called SeaGen, was the first of its kind. Looking like an upside-down windmill, it was designed to produce **electricity** from tides. Britain has the best tide and wave energy resources in the world. These sources could provide one-fifth of the country's electricity.

This machine uses the flow of the tides to create electricity.

WORD BANK

efficient effective and not wasteful

tide natural rising and falling motion in the world's seas

Sunlight

Without the Sun's **energy**, there would be no life on Earth. Happily, the Sun will probably last for another five billion years. It is a **renewable** energy source.

Heating water

There are several ways we can turn sunlight into useful energy. The simplest method is to place containers of water in strong sunshine. Some houses have a system of flat plates with water pipes running through them. The water absorbs (takes in) the Sun's heat. This water is pumped away and stored for future use. More cold water is then run into the pipes.

A much bigger heating system can use this method. Huge mirrors reflect the Sun's light to a single spot. This creates enormous heat. This system is used to boil water and create steam. The steam turns a **turbine**, creating **electricity**.

Panels with PVCs have to be kept very clean. This allows them to receive the full power of the Sun.

Turning light into power

Special devices called **photovoltaic cells (PVCs)** turn the energy of the Sun's **rays** into electricity. Sets of PVCs can be set up to follow the movement of the Sun. PVCs are very useful in far-off places where there is no major energy source— for example, in mountains, deserts, or out at sea.

Special panels are fitted to the roofs of many new houses in sunny areas. The panels help people use the Sun's energy.

What's the problem with solar energy?

Solar energy (the Sun's energy) is free and clean. There is plenty of it, and it is unlikely to run out. But there are problems:

- There is no Sun at night. What happens in the dark?

- Some areas of the world get almost no Sun in winter.

- Better ways of storing solar energy need to be invented.

- PVCs are very expensive.

What would YOU do ?

How would you solve the problems posed by solar energy? Look at websites such as www.facts-about-solar-energy.com/facts-about-solar-energy.html for some ideas.

WORD BANK
photovoltaic cell (PVC)   special device that changes the energy in the Sun's rays into a flow of electricity

33

Local power

Heating panels like **PVCs** make it possible for everybody to create **electricity** at home. Single households or small communities could decide to produce their own power locally. They would not need enormous **power stations** or power lines. This electricity would not produce **carbon**. It would not damage the **environment**.

Solar cities

Across the world, many cities have set goals to use **solar energy**. None will be fully Sun-powered for at least 10 years. These "solar cities" include Adelaide and Perth, in Australia, and Rizhao, in China. In 2009 the country of India announced plans to increase use of solar energy in 60 cities (see the box at right).

What would YOU do ?

Would you like your local city to become a solar city? Find out more about what this means. Look at www.bettergeneration.com/solar-cities-around-the-world.html for ideas.

People can use solar energy at home.

India's first solar city

In India, the city of Nagpur is being developed as that country's first solar city. **Renewable** energy sources will provide 10 percent of its **energy**. Solar energy systems will be installed. These will include streetlights, traffic lights, and solar water heaters. Energy-**efficient** buildings will also be promoted.

The central government will pay half of the cost. State or local governments will provide the rest. The Indian government plans to develop 60 such cities during a five-year plan.

Several cities in Asia produce most of their electricity from renewable sources.

Fuels from plants

Plants need sunlight to grow. These plants give us **energy** when we eat them. But the stored energy of some plants can be turned into a different kind of energy. They can be made into **fuels** called **biofuels**.

In one method of making biofuels, fast-growing woody plants such as poplar trees are grown. They are then ground into chips and burned in a **power station**. This creates **electricity**. In a second method, the oils or sugars from plants such as sugarcane are turned into fuel. This fuel, called **biodiesel**, can be used to power vehicles.

Woody plants can be chopped into tiny pieces. They are then used as fuel in power stations.

Miscanthus

A biofuel called miscanthus (or "elephant grass") has received a lot of attention lately. This fast-growing plant is used to make a gasoline substitute or a fuel for power stations. If people use it instead of fossil fuels, it could prevent **carbon dioxide** from being released.

But growing biofuels means there will be less land for growing food. We will need to grow much more food in the future, not less. Do research on biofuels and find out:

- How much farmland is now being used to grow biofuels?
- How many people in the world face a food shortage?
- What are other ways to grow biofuels using the Sun's power?

Miscanthus is a very fast-growing plant used to make biofuels.

WORD BANK

biodiesel   fuel made from natural oils. It is similar to the diesel fuel used by vehicles like trucks.

biofuel   fuel made from the stored energy of some plants

Less Waste, Less Energy

We have looked at the main types of **energy** we can use. But we cannot continue using them all. Some, like **fossil fuels**, are causing major damage to our **environment**. Others, like wind energy, need to be developed more before they can take over. But how can we bridge the **energy gap**?

Saving energy

One solution is to burn less of the energy that we do have. That way, it will last longer and cause less damage to the environment. We have to make cars that use less **fuel**. Our buildings have to be **insulated** with protective layers. This means heat will not leak out. Lights and electronic equipment in factories, stores, and homes have to be used less often. New materials and techniques have to be developed to be more **efficient**.

This eco-house has a grass roof. It is built partly underground, to stop heat loss.

Inside an eco-house

An **eco-house** is a house designed to save energy. It is made from **renewable** materials that create no **pollution**. It uses water, **electricity**, and other resources as efficiently as possible.

Most of us, of course, live in ordinary homes. Yet most houses can be made more environmentally friendly. For example, you can insulate roofs and walls to keep heat in. Or you can replace old lightbulbs with new energy-saving ones.

Some modern homes are designed to do very little damage to the environment.

WORD BANK
eco-house house designed to save energy and create little pollution
insulate add layers to a house to keep the inside at an even temperature

39

More ways to save energy

Here are some more **energy**-saving ideas:

- *Pavement power*
  In France, in the city of Toulouse, people's feet will press down special pavement slabs. This will make enough energy to power the streetlights.

- *Cow manure*
  In 2002 the United Kingdom opened a **power station** powered by cow dung (waste). The station burns methane, the **gas** given off by the dung. The cows of 30 farms provide enough power to light 900 homes.

- *Giant kites*
  A U.S. company plans to build a huge kite. This will fly above big ships. It will help haul them along. The company thinks this will save up to 20 percent of normal **fuel** usage.

Solutions big and small

On page 41, two case studies show that saving energy can work. One is about a big company that operates throughout the world. The other is about a small, local one. Both have made big efforts to bridge the **energy gap**. They are using **renewable** resources. They are also cutting down on the damage they cause to the **environment**.

The ship *MS Beluga Skysails* was the first cargo ship to be partly powered by a kite.

Dell

The computer company Dell set a goal to be one of the "greenest" companies on the planet. ("Green" means causing little damage to the environment.) Dell has worked to reduce the amount of **carbon** its products release. Dell also plans to **recycle** its products (such as laptop computers) at its 1,500 U.S. stores. Recycling means turning something into a new product.

Many parts from old computers can be removed and used again in new products.

The Chipper

In 2009 a British company called First Bus began to use the Chipper. This is a bus that can run on 100 percent **biodiesel** fuel. This fuel is made from leftover cooking oil. This greatly cuts down the amount of carbon **emissions**. The company relies on donations of oil to keep the bus going. A number of businesses in the city have provided oil. Everyday people have also given their own used cooking oil.

WORD BANK
recycle   reuse something (such as garbage) so it can be turned into a new product

Energy: The Final Verdict

It is time to decide. How will you bridge the **energy gap**? Which kinds of **energy** will serve the world best in the coming century?

Take a look at the sample tables on these pages. Then create your own. Give each type of energy a mark between 10 (the best) and 0 (the worst) in each category. How do they compare?

The Local Impact

Energy source	Cost	Sustainability	Reliability	Safety	Other effects	Total
Fossil fuels	8	5	6	2	1	22
Coal	6	3	6	3	2	20
Oil						
Natural gas						
Nuclear energy						
Renewables						
Wind energy						
Hydroelectric energy						
Wave energy						
Biofuel						
Solar energy						

The column "Sustainability" lets you assess whether the energy source can continue to be used over time. The column "Other effects" gives you the chance to think how your choice will affect people. For example, if we close coal **mines**, what happens to out-of-work miners? And what about poorer countries that have rich supplies of coal?

Finally, you can add up the scores and find the winners. The table on page 42 is about the local impact of your energy choices. The table on this page shows how your decision will affect the world.

The Global Impact

Energy source	Cost	Sustainability	Reliability	Safety	Other effects	Total
Fossil fuels	7	5	6	2	2	22
Coal	5	2	3	2	2	14
Oil						
Natural gas						
Nuclear energy						
Renewables						
Wind energy						
Hydroelectric energy						
Wave energy						
Biofuel						
Solar energy						

Glossary

atom smallest unit that makes up everything on Earth

biodiesel fuel made from natural oils

biofuel fuel made from the stored energy of some plants

carbon substance in the air that leads to global warming

Carbon Capture and Storage (CCS) system in which carbon dioxide is taken out of waste gases from coal power stations. It is then pumped deep underground and stored.

carbon dioxide colorless gas that is a major cause of climate change

chemical energy energy made by burning—for example, by burning coal

clean energy energy source that is renewable and causes little damage to the environment

climate change change in patterns of temperature, rainfall, or wind. This can be caused naturally or by human actions.

dam structure that holds back the flow of water

deposit store or supply

eco-house house designed to save energy and create little pollution

efficient effective and not wasteful

electrical energy energy made by the flow of electric charges

electricity flow of energy that powers machines, streetlights, and more

emission giving off of dirty gases or other materials

energy ability to do work

energy gap situation in which we cannot produce enough power for our needs

environment natural world on Earth

extract remove

fertilizer solid material sprinkled on farmland to make crops grow

fossil remains of an ancient plant or animal

fossil fuel fuel such as coal, oil, or natural gas formed from the remains of ancient plants and animals

fuel substance that can be used to create energy

gas substance without a definite shape, like air

generator machine that produces electricity

global warming rise in the temperature of Earth

grid central source of electricity that sends it to everyone in a large area

harness use the power of something

hydroelectric energy energy created when the power of moving water is used to turn a turbine and create electricity

Industrial Revolution period in history from the late 1700s through the 1800s, when factories and machines came into use in places like Great Britain and the United States

insulate add layers to a house to keep the inside at an even temperature

kinetic energy energy made by movement, such as wind or waves

mine area deep within Earth where people dig for substances such as coal; also, the act of digging in a mine

natural gas fuel gas found naturally in the ground

nuclear energy energy made by splitting the nucleus (central part) of a uranium atom

nucleus central part of an atom

photovoltaic cell (PVC) special device that changes the energy in the Sun's rays into a flow of electricity

pollution harming the environment with poisonous or dangerous substances

population number of people in an area

potential energy energy made by using natural forms of energy that are stored

power station place where energy is created

radiation energy in the form of rays

radioactive giving off radiation (harmful rays)

ray line or beam of energy

recycle reuse something (such as garbage) so it can be turned into a new product

renewable fuel or material that can be grown or made again (such as plants from seeds)

solar energy energy from the Sun

tide natural rising and falling motion in the world's seas

turbine machine turned by flowing energy, such as water, that changes this energy into electricity

uranium substance that is used to create nuclear reactions

Find Out More

Books

Benduhn, Tea. *Solar Power* (*Energy for Today*). Pleasantville, N.Y.: Weekly Reader, 2009.

Fridell, Ron. *Earth-Friendly Energy* (*Saving Our Living Earth*). Minneapolis: Lerner, 2009.

Green, Jen. *Why Should I Save Energy?* (*Why Should I?*). New York: Barron's Educational Series, 2008.

Guillain, Charlotte. *Reusing and Recycling* (*Help the Environment*). Chicago: Heinemann Library, 2008.

Leedy, Loreen. *The Shocking Truth About Energy*. New York: Holiday House, 2010.

Morris, Neil. *Saving Energy* (*Green Kids*). Mankato, Minn.: QED, 2009.

Peppas, Lynne. *Ocean, Tidal and Wave Energy: Power from the Sea* (*Energy Revolution*). New York: Crabtree, 2009.

Walker, Niki. *Generating Wind Power* (*Energy Revolution*). New York: Crabtree, 2007.

Woodford, Chris. *Energy* (*See for Yourself*). New York: Dorling Kindersley, 2007.

Websites

www.eia.doe.gov/kids
This website for kids offers lots of information about different energy sources.

www.energysavers.gov
This website tells you how to save money while making your home more environmentally friendly.

www.ecokids.ca
This website offers games, stories, pictures, and facts about the environment.

www.iea.org
The website of the International Energy Agency is a good source for facts and figures.

www.neok12.com/Energy-Sources.htm
Find videos, quizzes, lessons, and games about different energy sources.

http://tiki.oneworld.net/energy/energy.html
This is an energy guide for kids, with links to other energy sites.

Movies

The Eleventh Hour (2008).
This movie, starring Leonardo DiCaprio, documents the dangers facing many of the planet's life systems.

An Inconvenient Truth (2006).
This film was part of former U.S. Vice President Al Gore's campaign to publicize the dangers of global warming.

The Truth About Climate Change (2008).
The famous naturalist David Attenborough travels the world to find shocking evidence of climate change.

Index